For Kids and Grandkids Throughout the World

Zoo Nonsense
copyright © 2009 by
Don Clifford and Olga Cruhm

First Step Publishing Company
2101 E. Bowie Ave
Harlingen, TX 78550

A

There once was a chubby Armadillo,
Who was a nice quiet sort of fellow.
He would grub up a few bugs,
Or munch on some slugs,
But never had a taste for jello.

There once was a Big, Brawny Buffalo,

Who stood tall and tuff-alo.

He would give you the eye

Until you said "Bye,"

Then he'd walk off in a huff-alo.

There once was a Cheetah named Chigger

Who used his nose and toes to figger.

He would add up a sum

For which the outcome

Was always some figger bigger.

Now, poor Chuck was a Duck
Who ran out of luck
When his flippers got stuck in the muck.

He flapped very hard,
But he flapped in vain,
And he soon got mired
In the gooey terrain.

But Chuck, with luck,
Got unstuck with a truck.

Once there was an Elephant who forgot

That a swinging monkey he was not.

He would hang by his trunk

Until he slipped - kerplunk!

Right into a stink pot.

There once was a Ferret named Farley

Who waltzed a chipmunk named Marley.

Oh, how they danced and they dipped,

Until he slipped and they tripped.

Poor Farley lost Marley

To a cool cat named Charlie.

My neck is so long
I get hooked on a prong
When I stick my head in a tree.

If I had a snout
I could splash with a shout,
But only a Giraffe I be.

There once was a vain Hippopotamus,

Who itched on her tickly vast bottomus.

When she reached back to scratch

Her foot tripped in thatch

And her bottomus up-ended on top of us!

There once was a weary Iguana
Who wandered his way from Tijuana.
He could flick off a fly
Without batting an eye.
But when offered a bug
He would back off and shrug,
..."I don't wanna."

There once was a foxy old Jaguar

Whose mother had named him Farquar.

He would sit in a tree

From which he could see

His lunch trot in from afar.

Oh so sad was the sad Kangaroo,
Who sat on her tail in the dew.
Her legs were quite stumpy,
Her pouch was plain lumpy...
She really had nothing to do.

There once was a great pride of Lions

Who took great pride in their environs.

Whenever they'd eat

They would rinse off their feet

And use garbage bags with the tie-ons.

When Mongo the Monkey swings on a vine,

He does it with care and ever so fine.

If he were to fumble

He's likely to tumble

On top of a fat porkypine.

There once was a Newt named Newton

Who would toot on a flute uncertain.

But people upstairs

Thought Newt put on airs

When he danced about rooty-toot-tootin.

Orville was a nervous Orangutang

Who flipped about and sprang

To any old tree

Which had a branch free,

But always flipped back like a boomerang.

There once was a Porcupine named Pickles

Who liked lots of giggles and tickles.

But on his birthday

He got carried away

And...oops! He got stuck on his stickles.

Once there was a wierd bird named Qale

Who was one part rooster

And the other part Quail.

When it came time to fly,

He could not launch high,

So he would send himself air mail.

There once was a horny-faced
Rhinocerous
Who sipped tea from a cup and a
Saucerous.
He tried to explain
But it was obviously plain
That a saucerous was simply
Preposterous.

THERE ONCE WAS A SKUNK NAMED SNUFFY,

HIS SMELLY OL' TAIIL WAS SCRUFFY.

HE WOULD CLEAN AND HE'D PREEN,

AND THEN EAT A SARDINE

"TILL HIS TAIL WAS NICE AND FLUFFY.

Deep in the jungles of Niger,

There roamed a big and ferocious Tiger.

He went on a diet.

To make his Tum quiet,

He slurped a big spoon of vinegar.

The Unicorn is a mythic beast.
One day while enjoying a feast
Of new mown cloverleaf hay,

A wizard came by and said, "Boo!"

This so scared the beast
That he fled to the East,
And no one knows where, to this day.

Now, Velma was a Vampire bat

Who lost a button from her hat.

She flit to look here; she flit to look there.

It wasn't here, nor was it there.

Because it fell under a gnat.

There once was a Warthog named Willie

Who dashed about so crazy and silly.

He'd get on a bus,

Then make a big fuss

And ride around Willie-nillie.

X marks the spot
Where you can stand a lot
Wond'ring if you are here or there.
If you are not here,
Then you are there,
And elswhere you are not.

Once there was a Yak named Yancy

Who had a best friend named Clancy.

They would race up a hill

And then take a bad spill,

'Cause Yaks are simply not fancy.

There once was a Zebra named Ziggie
Who grazed in the grass like a piggie.
On every third day
He ate nothing but hay
Until he got baggy and biggie.

THE WORKS
By Don Clifford

The Trilogy; *Ben Solomon in:*
        Destiny Diverted
        The Quest for Kuybera
        The Return:

Children's:
        Zoo Nonsense
        More Zoo Nonsense
        Squeaky, the Littlest Angel
        A Kid's History of Brownsville (Texas)

Anthologies:
        The Hitching of Bingo Joe to the
            Widow Wheatley
        The Rio Grande: A River With
            A Thousand Tales
        Collected Tales from the Rio Grande
        A Blast From The Past; Two Volumes

Privately Published:
        The Life and Times of Robert Kane
        One Clifford Family From Ireland

www.ingramcontent.com/pod-product-compliance
Lightning Source LLC
Chambersburg PA
CBHW040347060426
42445CB00029B/25